MEANWHILE, TREES

Mark Waldron was born in New York. He grew up in London where he now lives with his wife and son. He began writing poetry in his early 40s and published two collections with Salt, *The Brand New Dark* (2008) and *The Itchy Sea* (2011). His third collection, *Meanwhile, Trees*, was published by Bloodaxe in 2016. *The Brand New Dark* was chosen for the Poetry Book Society's Next Generation Poets promotion in 2014.

Mark Waldron

Meanwhile, Trees

BLOODAXE BOOKS

ISBN: 978 1 78037 296 9

First published 2016 by
Bloodaxe Books Ltd,
Eastburn,
South Park,
Hexham,
Northumberland NE46 1BS.

www.bloodaxebooks.com
For further information about Bloodaxe titles
please visit our website or write to
the above address for a catalogue.

Supported using public funding by
**ARTS COUNCIL
ENGLAND**

Cover design: Neil Astley & Pamela Robertson-Pearce.

Printed in Great Britain by Bell & Bain Limited, Glasgow, Scotland, on
acid-free paper sourced from mills with FSC chain of custody certification.

For my mum and dad

ACKNOWLEDGEMENTS

Some of these poems, or versions of them, have appeared in *Blue of Noon, Kaffeeklatsch, Magma, The Morning Star, Poetry London, Ploughshares, Poetry Wales, Rising, The Quietus* and *Transom Journal*. 'So I hid my song' was commissioned by Rachel Whiteread for her 2013 show at Gagosian in London. 'Denmark Brochure' and 'All my poems are advertisements for me' were published in *Follow the Trail of Moths* published by Sidekick Books. 'The Decline of the Long s', was written for *Likestarlings* in an exchange of poems with Jena Osman; 'The Sea' was commissioned by Jackie Saphra and Kate Potts for *Somewhere in Particular*; and 'A cat called Orangey was in a number of movies' was published by Sidekick Books in *Lives Beyond Us*. 'Collaboration' appears in *Best British Poetry 2013*, 'First off appears' in *Best British Poetry 2014*, and 'I am lordly, puce and done' appears in *Best British Poetry 2015*, all published by Salt.

I'd like to thank Roddy Lumsden, John Stammers, Ahren Warner and my wife, Julie Hill, for their advice and suggestions on these poems.

CONTENTS

9   So I hid my song

10   You know when you drop

11   All My Poems Are Advertisements for Me

12   Meanwhile, Trees

13   So I was at home doing the washing up

14   The Sea

15   The Madding Wind

16   When You Come in, Poppet

17   A train, pale white in colour,

18   Look at Our Faces – How Dead We're Going to Be!

19   The Shoes of a Clown

20   A cat called Orangey was in a number of movies,

21   The Uncertainty Principle

22   You know that intermingled time of night and day

23   The Fire

24   Uh-Oh Sweet Wife

25   As Though We Hoped to Be Forgiven

26   A Glib

27   Yes I admit that I have ate

28   King Richard I

29   Confessional Poem

30   The Meeting

32   Poem in which

33   Innovations in Naval Gunnery

34   Underground Beekeeping

35   Vegetable Magnetism

36   Outdoor Philately

37   No Moose

38   Sucked

39   Sometimes a Phallus Is Just a Phallus

40   The Dead Are Helpless

41   The Voice

42   Those worms that inhabit the bowel,

43   In the Boulangerie

44   Guns in Films

45 *It's hard to see Hamlet as some kind of everyman,*

46 The Decline of the Long s

47 No More Mr Nice Guy

48 Professor Hydrofoil Is Attending a Matinee

50 The Tenant

51 We rested our hands

52 Grace

53 Manning

54 I Collaboration

55 II The Stage Is Set

57 III Does a Filmic Wind Tousle the Photo-Real Grass?

60 IV Denmark Brochure

61 V Manning in the Rock Garden

62 VI Out Here in the Future, Everything Is Doubly Suspect

64 VII *I am lordly, puce and done,*

65 VIII *Don't talk to me about ghosts,*

74 IX Enter a Ghost Smelling Minty

75 The Common Quail

77 The Lawn Sprinkler

78 First off,

So I hid my song

in a disused shed. No wait, that's not right, first I hid
my song in a tin,

and then the tin I hid in a sock, and the sock in a shoebox,
and the shoebox in a hatbox, and the hatbox

in the box that the breadbin came in.
So I concealed that box among a rummage of others

of hundreds of sizes and sounds-when-you-shook-them,
in that shed above-mentioned.

And I'd begun to walk away when I turned and I saw
that the shed was all lit with the sun,

and I resolved there and then that I must squirrel the shed
under the ground in a dilapidated field

where dirt grew and ephemera lay scattered about
like butter.

And once I'd buried the shed then I hid the whole field
in the blue-red mountains,

sliding it into a slot that I'd made beneath trees and foxes
and ants.

And then those mountains I shoved, like that, upside down
in the sopping wet bed of the sea,

and the sea I secreted beneath a particular sky, and the sky
under space,

and space I buried beneath that pernickety edge of nothing.
And now it's still not safe.

You know when you drop

something, a bottle or a vase perhaps, and when it first
contacts the ground it does so in such a state of shock

that it pauses there stunned, just for a fraction of
a moment, before it comes to, and expeditiously collects

itself, summons, despite its near panic, a sense
of obligation, recalls just what's expected of it, before it

tenses its body, scrunches up its eyes, fabricates
from nothing an explicit *pop* and a mass escape

from the suffocating incarceration of existence,
a breakout that dashes obediently to its slot, that being

the ordained scatter-pattern of pieces and bits, where it rests
then in an array of elfin smiles that seem to celebrate relief,

to relish languidly what they, for this moment, take to be their
liberty and to smoke thin cigarettes with their small feet

up in front of TVs showing film of countryside in Spring,
the next cell door having not yet swung entirely shut.

All My Poems Are Advertisements for Me

When I was young there was nothing exactly stupid
about the world. In fact, in the good old days

there was the thump and the tug of it, the way it heaved itself
like a stone, yanked so to speak in glory,

the way it fell up, crushed up, and then crushed up again,
getting newer and newer, louder and sweeter,

the way it watched its own face fall between its fingers
as though its face were a handful of gold coins.

I think I might have known the whole drag of everything
going upwards, a tide that pulled me with it.

Actually, I know I did. (You were part of all this by the way.)
And the sky, well, where to begin?

The sky was so adult, not imbecilic or thin or so-so or girlish.
Did I outgrow it?

Did I drink it, shoot it, find a way round it?
Did I get inside it and drive off in it?

Forgive me, but on my way to work this morning,
even though the sun was on fire and the trees were up,

I was in the apocalypse. Death is not what you think it is.
It's actually what I think it is.

Meanwhile, Trees

He was thinking, as he rocketed across the Tuileries,
top-hat steadied with one hand, cane gripped in the other,
and with that coddled little smile still (despite the haste
of the body that carried it!) goofing-off all nonchalant in
the otherwise deserted high-school corridor of his face, that
perhaps he might remake himself from something already
half-mutated such as a hotel pool-soaked novel or something
whose extra weight, as he would explain to Gaston later,
would be promissory, such as the lavish body of a maggot.

La scène: Paris, mil neuf cent dix. The city streets are wet
with an old-fangled rain that feels, rubbed between
contempo fingers, entirely *démodé*. It's winter and the trees
have done *avec* their leaves, have choked them at the wrist,
strangled every one until they each gave up their flat green
ghosts, turned a purplish black, and dropped just as the
rubber-banded barren nuts of rams drop and do germinate
not at all in no hot earth. Oh, how he hurries crispy under
branches, possessing, as he does, all the lightness of the lost!

So I was at home doing the washing up

and I thought, perhaps I'm using
too much washing up liquid. I actually
like to use a lot of washing up liquid
because I think it makes the work easier,
well that's the impression I get anyway,
but I have had the feeling that some
people think I use too much. I definitely
had the impression that my parents thought
I was using too much washing up liquid
when I was over at their house last week
and helping out after lunch. And then
today I thought, you know what, I can use
as much damn washing up liquid as I like
in my own damn house and no one can
stop me. I could squirt the whole of this
bottle straight down the drain if I felt like it,
and if my wife said what the heck are you
doing, I could just smile at her and carry on.
In fact no one could stop me if I sold
the damn house and everything in it
and spent all the money I got from
the sale on washing up liquid. I could
have it delivered in tankers if I could get
the parking permits. I'm appalled that
I could actually do that and no one could
have me arrested because after all it's my
damn money. How the hell is that kind
of thing allowed to happen? Someone really
needs to have the authority to intervene
and protect me from myself.

The Sea

The man and his small dog performed their shuffling dance.
The crinkly suit the man wore was designed to mimic the sea,
his made-up face too was greyish blue and his mouth, a wet
cave that uttered the crunchy sounds of the sea as well as *fish*
and *crab* and *anemone*. His hair was white and coiffed in
the style of foam. The man and his dog moved purposefully
towards the audience then paused and reversed back again
in the fashion of waves. He comprehended his role but his
little white poodle in its blue coat only followed, as waves
blindly follow their predecessors towards a jaded shore.

On holiday last month I was entertained by the action
of the actual sea. Each wave that broke upon the rocks
at Morte Point was its own show. Each wave struck its pose
and then withdrew, grand and throwaway, tossed off
with the nonchalance of a well-rehearsed performance,
yet always fresh and daring (or so it seemed to me) in its
improvised quality. The variation was infinite and ridiculous
and there was a distinct new-agey flavour to the whole splash,
as well as a consistent sense of something magically bogus,
a contrived simulacrum of revelatory meaning.

The Madding Wind

I stood on a path in the little park alone that afternoon
and I watched in my dismay the wind
as it threw all connotation out of the battered trees.

I saw it rake it from the grass, thresh it from the plants,
the stones, the little fence and the very sky itself,
so that the covenant each had

with its ancient reputation was beaten from it easily as seed
is hit from straw. That wind it blew allusion
right off of all creation, stripped it of its candied coat,

left nothing but a brittle chaff that danced depraved
and godless jigs with it. And when I turned myself
towards the blow I knew at once my face it emptied

like an upturned sugar bowl to make a hollowed
thrown-down countenance, and I found myself conjoined
with that divested little park in its perverted dance.

When You Come in, Poppet

Your cold clothes. Your cheek against mine,
stiffened with a thrilling foreign chill
you've picked up outside.

Well I move back in ahead of you.
I arrange my papers like this
on the kitchen table and I sip my tea once or twice.

Of course I must take you
back into the melting warm. I must take you
all the way in again and shove

and shove out
what I can of the whole day,
that spruced-up bull that's left its cleanly

trace in you, that smart day
with its fearless strut and its white clothes
like the white clothes of a saint.

A train, pale white in colour,

stopped beside a bleary field at dusk, leaks
its waspish steam in wisps that eke from pistons,
slits and pipes. On board the train there sits
a little man within whose leather bag there is,
well wrapped in rags, a disembodied folded leg
that's formed of tiny epidermis-fronted drawers
every one of which is so precisely made no
evidence of it is seen upon the surface of the skin.
Each drawer he has constructed out of flesh,
and each contains a tidy portion of it that fills it
to its brim. Just as a wily counsel might press
his point and thus unbolt a box in which a voice
is locked, so might this passenger press artfully
enough upon a section of the limb that it will click
somewhere deep within its meat, somewhere near
its marrow, with a knock like a muffled penny's
drop, and with a subtle jolt will spring against
his finger's nudge before it saunters smoothly out
lubricated solely by the goodness of its fit.
It will follow his retreating digit to present
its content, hidden within the folds of which
is the modest smell of it. And then at once,
with but a fraction of a pause, the drawer will
pop coquettish back inside its slot unprompted
by a push as though suddenly ashamed it had
displayed itself and all the neatness of its butchery.

Look at Our Faces – How Dead We're Going to Be!

It's the abundance of specificity that leaves me
so dying.

I go hotfoot through miserable woods that are haunted
by me, and here are the trees

each of whose leaves suggests its particular green.
I walk across a field

that's been spattered with fragments of cow shit
every bit of which is specific.

Here are bones, buttons. Here are wild dogs, biscuits,
French horns, imps, borlotti beans.

Here is a submarine, a brick, a rose hip.
Here are the piping bodies of girls and boys once popped

like perfect peas from puberty's cramped pupa;
basted, they gleam head to toe with poem juice.

And here are all the world's small stones arranged
in order of roughness with the smoothest on the right.

The Shoes of a Clown

Oh, how I'd love to own a pair of those
long-toed clown shoes. I think I would find myself so engaging
in them. I'd put them on, sit down upon a chair, reach out my legs
in front of me, and happily behold my oddly-shod feet. I'd stand
and slap their long lengths on the ground to generate a flapping sound,

a flapping sound like a crack. Like a *Crack! Crack!* And then I'd hurry
up to see you, I would hurry backwards up the stairs to show you
my two new shoes, and you'd turn round and apprehend my self
emerging up from them, a genie drifting from its polished lamp,
a plant sucking at its just watered ground.

A cat called Orangey was in a number of movies,

but he didn't know he was. He didn't even know
he was in *Breakfast at Tiffany's*.

Obviously he knew nothing about it. All he registered
were the peculiar new locations, the heat of the lights,

and a vague sense of fear, as well as bursts of affection
coming from the people around him.

Of course cats know just about nothing
of the human world at all.

They live in a parallel universe *inside* the human world.
Mostly smaller than it and fitting into it,

though in places its boundaries stretch beyond
the boundaries of our experience in soft tubular fingers.

Their consciousness would be repellent to us if we could
inhabit it.

Its lack of words and its meat and the fur that we might
experience as being in our mouths.

The paucity of its dimensions, that flatness, would press us
to the ground, make our heads split.

The configuration of their genes is such that they would
bring us down,

would make us blind to everything that from up here
we are able to see,

and open up, at last, a sharp slick world full of certainty
and ease of feeling.

The Uncertainty Principle

I wouldn't swear to it but it seems to me that light owns
the surfaces of things,
dotting them indiscriminately with its capricious particles.

pok! pok! pok!
pok-pok! pok-pok-pok! pok! pok!

Each, a paintball pellet which,
on splatting, contributes to colour-up the ravenous darkness
rendering it fit for purpose.

That purpose being
to be seen.

I admit I memorised whole portions of you
and under various lighting conditions. I made a bit of a project of it.

There were particles everywhere! An embarrassment of riches!

You held out your hands palms-up
and you smiled at me as they rained down on you like dolphins.

I find it very hot the way particles exist so saucily in two places
at once, don't you?

Your nipples, if I might say so, have something of that quality,
upon their quantum hooters.

pok! pok!

I would shut out my black mouth if I could.
Not everything
is explicable. Exemplar: I know what I mean. Or I think I do.

You know that intermingled time of night and day

when the sun un-sets, and vanilla wakefulness is still
somewhat subservient to sleep's dirty kingdom?

Well there I was, inside some 16th century Padua
and I watched agog

as pretty maids in period underclothes scampered
laughing down a palace's back stairs;

and on those stairs, wedged pressed against a wall
between the ceiling and the floor,

there stood but one enormous Pop-Tart,
napalm hot it was and leaking its delicious sticky milk.

Un-boned, the maidens pulled their smocks away
apparently instinctively as though the tart

were stationed there every time they went that way.
I mention this small curio because it's surely you

that is the piping tart and me that's all the lovely girls,
nimble-toed, contriving with each circuit

some concealed way that one of them might trip,
and in her falling, send them all a-tumble into it.

The Fire

The busbied sticks, they lay to strict attention
in their box till he struck one awake
and its hat blurted out its clutch of light.
Soon he let the infant fire begat
of that quick friction off the tip
of its blackening and cringing match
as one might coax a brilliant beetle off
one's finger to a leaf.
And the reluctant flame it left
the shrivelled stick that it had sucked
of all its sticky milk of flammability,
and there it hung on paper's edge,
dangled upwards, lingered shyly
on the threshold of its lot.
That ingratiating flame looked back
at his hot face to see if he might
really let it go, if he might let it pick up
its proper clean heat like skirts and run
and rummage wantonly,
laughing and ripping at its own clothes,
distraught with all its joy.
And he did let it riot, he let it dance
and swear such smart filth
as druids did on Mona's shore
before the panicked Romans slaughtered them.

Uh-Oh Sweet Wife

So, you bust us in flagrante,
me and my other beloved, myself and my infinite
intimate, the world, my mistress world.

Forgive me, but when she lays down her glittery
and genteel fuselage softly in my lap
I find that I must ruffle and placate her immensity.

For thus enthroned she alludes to all of this existence
that must condense
in drips upon the laminate surface of the vernacular.

And when I, tiring of my duty, rise,
I find the world
she goes where I go for we are ditto – she and me,

she is the ground, she is the tree, the branch, the leaf,
the scribbled nest in which I lay
so many times each hour my mottled eggs of breath;

my sucked eggs, my blown
and subtle eggs that whistle like an owl's seductive
song and have but one aim, to wit,

to woo her and then to lead her to the orchard floor
on which, with the dim-shod night, we'll creep.

As Though We Hoped to Be Forgiven

The trees don't lie down to sleep,
don't slump and break a slow

and hazardous recline, don't reach out
to take the first cautious little weight

with twigs and thinner branches,
and then their stolid tons

of sombre lumber with the thicker ones.
They don't bend at bark-split knee

to crunch and snap towards the unmade
rumpled ground, and then don't stack

their leaves neatly one upon another
as we lay our hands

in meagre piles beneath our pillows in that
vestigial indicium of prayer.

A Glib

You know how glib everything can be? I hate that. I hate how
glib things can be. You know, like:
'the dark is in the trees'.

What, as in, actually *in the trees?* (I despise italicised trees,
bent as though blown in westerlies.)

When I said, 'you know how glib everything can be,'
I think I knew what 'glib' meant.

But now I'm not sure,
because 'glib', it seems, has shed its meaning.

And what a charming little word 'glib' is
now that it's dropped its itchy carapace, now it's abandoned
its tiresome catchphrase.

Also, what a delightful little combo of words 'glib is' is.
I could go on.

I keep a glib in my shoe.
Just kidding,
I keep a glib in my walnut

Edwardian cabinet, where it belongs;
in with the other items that emanate whimsical sounds when
you warm them, like the quavering ringtones

of obsolete cell-phones, or the summoning clicks
of extinct insects, or the off-notes whistled
by sailors on whaleboats. I love that kind of thing.

I am charmed, of course, in the way that a critter is suddenly,
and just for a moment, sunlit.
I am charmed for a bit, and I hate it.

Yes I admit that I have ate

that once cool and heavy egg that would
one day have hatched a clever goose of gold.

I cooked it in a pan until it smelted from a hard
into a runny yolk,

and then I promptly drank the molten yellow,
gulped it down and felt it start to burn away

my tongue and gums and teeth whose residue
then blew away as smoke. I felt it coursing down

my roasting throat, through the squiggle
of my blistered viscera,

all the way beyond my screaming shitter
from which it oozed and swarmed and spread

wet metal excrement about my seared balls
and buttocks, before it slowly made to thicken.

And once I'd died of pain, then some time
afterwards I ate away my flesh and bone:

I sank my corpse in acid till no bit of it remained
but just this shiny winding cast, this meandered

single golden sprue that rises from its golden stand,
and displayed like this so well describes a fool.

King Richard I

The Richard the Lionheart poem that I have in my mind
exists so far only in discrete clumps that are like patches
of sunlit ground in an ancient, abstruse and deciduous forest.
These patches are anointed by an oily sunlight and a warmth
that the sunlight brings with it. Creatures large and small
are drawn here, from deer to boar, through rabbits to beetles
and midges; drawn both to the glistening patches of ground
with their macro abandon, and to the love-buttered air
that's dolloped above them, so that everything teems
with a fecund and sparkling plenty like loss.

Richard's place in the undergrown whole is as that
of an odour, a taste, no more than a presumptuous mood.
His impalpability, it appears aloof in its lack of concern
for the nebulous world which surrounds it. It's as though
the king rode through the forest with Captain Mercadier,
both vaporous men wearing unresearched costume,
both ignoring the fauna and flora and the flicker of light in
the leaves; or as though he picked at his as yet unborn teeth
in a manner befitting a foetus, or stroked his astrakhan
beard that's still drenched in the juice of the womb.

Confessional Poem

Forgive me: I've been tempted to make use
of dissonance in an effort to resonate;

I've walked all over my principles
in day-glo flip-flops;

I've attempted to schmooze when I should
have been rough and abusive;

In the locked bathroom, I've allowed my id
to goose my poor ego, scarring it mentally;

I've papered over the cracks with more cracks
to obtain a 'crack effect'; I've admired the cut

of my own jib, juddering stiff on a wester;
I've planted weeds in other people's

gardens on purpose; I've pretended my eyes
are windows and got drunk

in a room behind them; I've pretended
everything's just terribly droll and awful.

The Meeting

Rooney and I are in a poolside duplex bungalow at the Delano, Miami. Rooney is so famous at this stage of his career he's almost handsome, his face, over the period of his fame, having come to partly redefine the parameters of beauty. We lounge exaggeratedly on the white sofas as though we were each an item of clothing discarded in a moment of ostentatious passion. Neither of us attempts to strike up conversation as we're both a bit intimidated by the minimalist vulgarity of the setting that makes us feel a sneaking sense of that nasty brand of paranoia which cocaine might induce. Perhaps it looks a little whimsical of me to have brought us together in this manner, but I believed that in this unfamiliar location our toddling souls might spy each other through cracks in the waxy fabric of the cultures in which the two of us (in common with all humanity) are swaddled; those cultures which, attracted to us since birth by the universal gravity of neediness, accumulate on our innocent spirits just as tumbling, lifeless rocks once did clump onto the baby earth to form this rounded grownup globe. I'd hoped that these agglomerations had not yet fully set, inhibited in doing so by the warming effect of the dilute but pervading narcissism I sensed in each of us (a quality so often to be found in centre forwards and poets (particularly those whose primary carer might have exploited them in infancy as a means by which to regulate their own self-esteem)), and selfishly I thought our sympathy for the other's shared predicament might spark some sorrow in me and that I might cry as a sad ghost might, revelling happily in his own rich sadness. After what seems a period of hours but perhaps was only minutes, Rooney hears what he takes to be rats behind the walls. The sound makes him think of the grinding together of rocks and that, I'm afraid, distracts me from this my purpose and reminds me of you, my angel, in that rock-pool in Corsica, and that, in turn, makes me think of Napoleon Bonaparte which brings to mind the Retreat from Moscow which makes me picture the frozen bodies of Frenchmen which makes me imagine the Russian spring thaw and of meat defrosting in a freezer because rats have chewed through the wires behind the skirtings against which faux Victorian skirts would have brushed in costume dramas, had we rented out our home to production companies who would have dragged cables up the stairs disturbing those rats beneath the boards where they've been chewing on wood in order to slow the advance of their eternally-growing teeth, just as Rooney must relentlessly wear down the sulking beast of his ambition on the frustratingly giving surfaces of football fields. Rooney gets up from his chair and walks towards the windows. He's lathered in sweet grace that's made of the love I have for a small boy who not so long ago lay in bed, and listened to milk bottles celebrate in tears a brand new sun.

Poem in which

Dieter (don't ask) says: 'What's it like on the moon Buzz?
What's it like on the moon? Is it like, a-drawn? Like with,
a-pencil?

What's it like on the moon Buzz? Tell us, tell us!'

'We left our detritus on it,' says Buzz miserably, 'we left
our preposterous colours.'

And Dieter looks neither plussed nor nonplussed.

'We left our flag on it,' Buzz continues, and he mumbles:
'and our shame,' and then even more quietly:
'We took a goddamn dump on it,'

and then he lowers his orange-tinted visor
with his chunky-gloved fingers and bows his head.

When Buzz does eventually look up, Dieter sees his own
reflection dressed in its earthling costume coming back

at him like an admonishment in the glass's delicious curve.

And then Dieter turns to me, and-and-and Buzz turns to me too,
the lickable-kissable bowl of that head of his
all leant up towards me.

He's smiling I think, a joyous full smile beneath the helmet's
atmosphere. What an impertinent fish he is,

looking up at a kindly though enormously hungry heron!

Innovations in Naval Gunnery

She never fired her batteries in rage, but did once demonstrate
their exactitude and range on a clear day, two miles out off
Lowestoft. The armour-piercing shells she lofted, tossed towards
the target of an oil tanker's rusting hulk were each disguised
as armchairs – realistic in their leather-covered button-backed
bulk, they tumbled through the air, dropping their cushions,
showing their seats, their backs, their crude undersides.
'Look there! See the little wheels! And there, and there again!'

cried the beguiled air that stood aside to shuffle in once more
behind each high-explosive chair, and smile and clap quick little
claps at the passage of this, no surely not mirage, but entrancing,
discombobulating kind of camouflage! (I never saw the guns
themselves, and can only venture a guess as to whether the barrels
were deeply grooved within, to accommodate those legs
and castor wheels, or whether, more probably no doubt, the legs
flipped out like fins on exiting the gun's single-nostrilled snout.)

The warship's hull was fashioned in the form of a vast and inside-
outed drawing room with décor late Victorian. The oversize, sea
spray spattered paper was a William Morris pattern; the enormous
pictures hung like fenders, swung in gilded frames, grinding arcs
and thumping on their giant walls with the tossing of the choppy
sea; they were genre pieces, chock-a-block with dogs and little girls
and sympathy. So the ship she had her inside walls faced outward
in a gesture of apparently unguarded openness, but which might,

just as likely, have been evidence of its opposite, or the opposite
of that, or the opposite of that. How cruel that she was sunk by
the bastard French before she could fire off a single armchair round
in her defence. How it pains me to imagine all the men and women
happily inside the ship before the hit, their faces lit by monitors or
reflected in the doorknob's vast expanse of brass as they polished it.
That knob, which even had it turned, would not have opened the
humongous door onto the drawing room and all this infinite vacuity.

Underground Beekeeping

There was a febrile buzz around *free range*
back in the day,

and didn't he know it!

That,
and Christopher Isherwood, and stippling.

Of course with Christopher it was always seafood,
seafood, seafood
after he went communist. It's funny

to recall how we got so properly lost
among the rock pools without moving a muscle.

Later, when push came to shove, he had
the dachshund put down because it snapped.

Vegetable Magnetism

He was partly German, so it turned out,
and that was certainly a plus, the Germans
being famously more grown-up

when it comes to such matters,
perhaps due to the increasing
frequency of avalanches

as the rolling hills give way to
mountains proper and that
invigorating piquancy spikes the air.

The young architect found his *kartoffelpuffers*
particularly captivating. She couldn't
get them out of her mind for love or money.

Outdoor Philately

Would you Adam and Eve
it, I picked up a fracture

on my way to collage.

It was a huge affair.
A kind of communal, cut-

up in the bibliothek with
the great and the good.

And there she was!

I broke my toe when I
stamped on
a baumstumph of all things.

Anyone
who's anyone was there

brandishing butterflies,

I mean incisors like calling
cards. Did I say butterflies?

No Moose

An English seaside town at dusk, warmth
radiated by the stone buildings, warmth
emerges like sunburnt evening promenaders
from the stone buildings, warmth is secreted
like a pheromone from the stone buildings,
warmth emanates like the warmth of
the breath of a monotone speech from
the stone buildings, streetlamps brighten
on a darkening sky, a middle-aged man bares
his teeth and cracks through the choc' of his
choc-ice, as an unfortunate explorer might
crack through the ice in the thaw on
the Hudson Bay, his lips stretched back in
a grimace of terror as he vanishes forever.

And there, in the chip shop, lit by its strip
lights, a cramped and uncomfortable moose,
its antlers brush ceiling, its head pushes hard
against counter, its twitching rump against wall
with informative pictures of fish. A moose in
a setting like this is like a dog in your pool,
perhaps not a vagrant in your bedroom sitting
on your pillow, or a noose in your playpen,
or sick on your patio, but a dog in your pool.
So remove it. Lit by the lights of the chippy, an
ordinary street; there's a man with a choc-ice,
the fading scent of a moose, the heartening
odour of vinegar, and the warmth given off
like a sigh of relief by the stone buildings.

Sucked

Sucked perhaps, and popped
from sockets, but still tethered
to the face by strings (as kites are
to their grounded flyers) the eyes
themselves won't cry, but their vacated
hollows might, the twin concavities
the tears fill until they, overflowing, spill.

So, two strung conkers now; portholed
bathyspheres which, both held between
a finger and a thumb, might each
be shown the bloated fish of the other.
These clackers, these sackless knackers,
this bolas which we gauchos use to hunt
on the scrubby plains of blindness.

Sometimes a Phallus Is Just a Phallus

(Interior. An earthy apartment.) This is how he puts it:
'I is properly done by the doubling, trebling or more
promise of my collected substance that jogs up to itself
in a like-minded, stiff congregation.'

'Pardon?' she says. 'What I *means* is,' he continues: 'that
all its serious/partly-comic wealth stumbles (not drunk
but not sober) onto the spot-lit stage of your cocked look.
The whole day is trumped. The sunlight on the sheets,

for example, is nearly in tears. So when I meets my
gathered dong, undressed in all its exquisite fine-grained
pomp, the stolid pleasure I draws in greets the pleasure
which the dong *itself* (my italics) accumulates, as aerials

pick up heavy tunes, or as money pulls down more money
to itself so furiously. Oops, it's coining it! It feels itself up,
my boner, and pumped on promise, it looms out of this
otherwise ordinary day as a charging horse crashes out

of a field, or as a bleeding hand reaches from the crumbly
grave, or sweet odour might bark (might it not?)
off the horny ground.' 'Oh, for God's sake, put it in,'
she whispers. And everything will be okay.

The Dead Are Helpless

You can do exactly what you want to the dead,
you can call them filthy names,
you can poke your uncovered arse at them,
you can stick them in the eye, or spit on them
or better, you could prop one up before you shove
its face backwards, your palm driven hard against
the nose, and still nothing bad will happen to you.

You can drag the dead outside into the street
and there you can piss upon them. You could beat
one even further into death with a brick and
no one can point a finger at you, and if they do
then you can tell them to fuck off and mock their
squeamishness by blubbing like a baby in mimicry
of the feebly sensitive.

(It occurs to me just now that you might also want
to stand a stiff in a doorway, have it held in place
by means of ropes and then with all your extant
vehemence, slam the door against it, hear it greet
the dead's unwincing face just before it bangs against
the jamb.) You can always confound the dead.
You can act as though you're going this way,

and then you can go that way and punch them,
and they'll just stare up at the ceiling with that
emptied look of theirs (emptied as an egg is from
its shell). And the dead have nothing at all to use
against you but your horror at their passivity
which looks sometimes so like the unresisting
sweetness of your own poor martyred soul.

The Voice

Its yellow/brown tones and its
vibration denote all the particular

fruit that the voice carries in its
wooden barrow. The voice

is a tired old emissary dressed in worn
and elaborate robes and sent out to trundle

by a small boy, a cocky prince
(though he has but the toy parts of a child,

not yet soused in tangled, romping spells).
The ground undulates beneath his

wooden wheel. The trees, they serve up
green on every platter. The inveigling

emissary is a cuckold whose wife
the royal squirt pleases enormously while

the emissary is out earning a crust and
smoothing out differences.

Those worms that inhabit the bowel,

they have their wives and husbands
and same-sex partners and children
who play in the park with Frisbees,
and scrape knees, and eat eggs or beans
for breakfast. They live in period homes
with creaky floorboards or in high-rise
apartments with views of the distant
fatherly hills. Those worms, they lace
up their shoes and go out to the shops,
buy jewellery and underwear and
cigarettes and spaghetti. They pop pills
at impromptu raves in car parks,
and go to classical concerts in rococo
halls. They drive cars, fly in aeroplanes,
take trains, climb trees and mountains,
work in marketing, lie in steaming hot
baths, let their gaze coalesce at their
artless toes, and wonder at the nature
of consciousness. Inwardly they chuckle
at the absurd, and sophisticated
thought that their vivid deep lives
might be nothing but projections.

In the Boulangerie

'God it exhausts me, trying to be elastic but safe
the whole time,' I whispered

when I bumped into myself, baguette in my hand,
at the back of the queue

in the touristy village in the hilly Dordogne,
'and also this attempting not to annoy, or attempting

to be just *somewhat* annoying in a manner
that gets people's goat in a way that their goat *enjoys*.'

I smiled the safe smile and, though I found
my manner affected, I understood perfectly

every word that I'd said. And despite being moved
by a hesitant sympathy I was, I admit,

just a little surprised by my age, my height, my weight,
the tone of my voice and my apparent torpidity

behind which, inside that additional time it accords me,
I found I was able to compose myself.

Guns in Films

Guns in films aren't like real guns, no siree.
For one thing we can love them wholeheartedly.

Also, unlike real guns that piss their banging stones,
guns in films are dirty only with our own delicious dirt.

So there's a 1970s Merc parked outside a petrol station
on a forest road. It's dusty and hot.
The car is a wunderbar greyish blue, yes, *that* blue.

A man in a black leather jacket of a type worn by Germans
in the 1970s and with a beard of the same period
points his automatic pistol at a man

in the Mercedes who ducks pathetically below the dashboard
and sucks at the last stupid bit of life down there.

The gun is a magnet that bends the fabric of the film
and draws everything flying towards it.

A gun in a movie is not the jam in a donut; it is the pip
in the jam in the donut, the jam being
the character's motivation, the dough being the script,

the donut's surface being the scene's location, and the sugary
coating being you in the cinema,
sprinkled-on-a-seat, wanting *everything*.

It's hard to see Hamlet as some kind of everyman,

bellows old Professor Hydrofoil above the sound of his own engine's biscuity shout as he skims across the pale Baltic waters lit with light. The sky is crazy for him, his riveted body, all chrome fuselage, instant abdomen and what looks from here to be a thing like kindliness. He is, in fact, so shiny, so polished by his mother's early love that we can observe ourselves reflected in his tubular skin. We can see our bent smiles which are the floaty grins of children who hold their parents' hands and watch the happy dogs who run through parks, throwing off their ridiculous beards and laughing, laughing, laughing. But wait! Prof Hydro's gone and got all serio'. He's docked himself in a study in an old house in Palookaville. He's donned huge human clothes. He looks out onto a cold wet street with the fallen leaves of trees stuck on it. The arrangement of the threads in his tweed jacket is such that that arrangement's own woollen heart is broken. On the radio is nothing because it's switched off.

The Decline of the Long s

Yes, perhaps it is just one example of a general
smoothening as we remove trip hazards; as we, in
cleansing everything, scrub down the surface of the
world, rub out the hills and fill the valleys with their
debris; as we, with rapid little kisses, kiss each other's
faces before we grind and bump, and by increments
inexorably breed away our distinct particularities; as we
deselect the differences in carrots; as we chop down
the trees; as we denude our hunkered genitals which
look up at us shamefacedly – exposed Viet Cong
bared to the hovering clatter of our glossy gaze
that hangs above their defoliated ground.

The triumph of the short s, that lesser letter,
represents an early contribution to this pervading
levelling as it can barely stick its tip above the sheen
that now lies spread like spread on the world's once
tantalising crevices and cracks. It plays its subtle part
as everything slips down and over us more nicely now.
My zipped-up inside is slick, it's spittled pretty as a
sucked-on lolly, and that's the womby state we ache to
have around us as well as in. Might I ask, did you spy
your own lubriciousness? Did you peruse your own
consoled reflection in it? Was your visage bouncing
back? Were you looking slippy? I rest my case.

No More Mr Nice Guy

This then,
what you actually witness here, before your
very eyelids, is an actual blooming waste of time, in action,

in real time. I squid you not, certain shall we say 'people'
with a certain shall we say 'cheek' have had a go at me about
punctuality & punctuation, specifically the use

or otherwise of ampersands & obscenities and rubbish
and whatnot. As well as my peculiar drinking and poking fun
at people with or without disabilities and so on.

Well from now on, from the very next thing I do onwards,
I'm going to do exactly as I blinking well please, which is to be
marvellously wretched & frightened and broken and hidden.

Professor Hydrofoil Is Attending a Matinee

It's a tight squeeze. The professor's brought in through the back of the theatre, and then with much ado is carried by a series of small cranes and pulleys across the stage, into the auditorium and finally, with the appearance of the Hindenburg Zeppelin, what with the stagehands steadying his movements by means of ropes, he's swung round by 180 degrees before he's lowered directly down onto the seating in the house. He rests across the stalls and occupies rows g, h, i, j, k, l and m and seats 2 to 23. Much to his embarrassment a number of them are badly damaged or even completely crushed beneath his weight, particularly those numbered 5 and 6, 20 and 21 in rows h, i, j and k. He's surprised that, having gone to such pains to get him into the theatre, the management should have done absolutely nothing to protect the seating! He's also mortified to discover that though the dress and upper circle sightlines are unaffected, his hull and superstructure obscure the view of all the people in rows n to w of the stalls, some of whom will attempt to catch something of the performance by clambering onto seats and trying to peer at the action through both sets of his windows. Soon, mercifully, the lights are lowered and in the dark he feels less self-conscious and able to relax a little, at least for a while that is. Being in this position means the professor's forced to view the performance by looking to one side, which he finds tiring and, in fact, he gives his eyes a break by letting them alight for short periods on a pale green exit sign directly ahead of him. He also has to suffer the uncomfortable sensation of resting on his foils without the support of water for a considerable period of time. It's hard to say whether the professor enjoyed the performance. In the same way as forcing oneself to smile induces the emotion normally associated with a smile, so the effect of watching the performance out of the corner of his eye generated in him a feeling of suspicious trepidation which he would forever associate with the performance he saw that night.

The Tenant

Pour drink out of a can, spoon
meat out of a tin:

air moves in. Some portion
of the air wakes up,

leaves its position
reclining dozily in space and drops

quick into every virgin crevice
of that fresh vacuity.

There it squats,
just as a hermit, crazy maybe

(inhabited by loss himself perhaps),
might squat a cave for forty years;

or as an undressed crab might haunt
a whelk's clockwise shell.

So that newly housed and hunkered
atmosphere, now it's made its home,

begins to brood and then to stew
that very spot it's in until

it's made of it a rich stock that is
the vivid ghost of that exact place.

We rested our hands

on the professor's back. I remember I could feel his unbending aluminium through the fabric of his jacket that, beneath our touch, slipped a bit against the shiny metal. That immalleable quality seemed so incongruous on him I almost recoiled and pulled away my hand earlier than would have seemed fitting. It's also true that I couldn't exactly tell if my touching of him was some conniving political gesture or if I'd genuinely meant it. I'm afraid that looking back, it seems that both might be true. Once you are aware of your effect, you will always be half dissembling. The professor didn't breathe or show any sign of life of course, though not because his life is some imaginary quality endowed on him by children. In fact I'd say the opposite was true. We had made him seem *not* to be alive, so that his sensational existence should be still more vivid every time it came to us.

Grace

One thing I like about collecting is that when I collect a thing
and add it to the bunch, then the pile outside the bunch diminishes

by precisely that amount. So effectively I disturb the world twice,
both intimately and broadly, both in privy, in my own shuttered

room, and also in the landscape beyond, with its indeterminate
scraping and shuffling and whooshing sounds. Also, when I make

my choice of object I radically alter its value allowing it to burst
from its cocoon of mundanity, its repulsive poverty, to emerge

soft and hot and beginning, almost vile in its shimmying vividity,
awoken by the anointing touch of just my poor bashful notice.

Effectively, I do well twice you see, and perhaps even a third time
in a kind of schadenfreude, because when I lifted the thing from

the pile outside, I denied it to my enemies who are many and
include all those solipsists with their nasty habits so aggrandised.

Manning

I don't know what Manning is, but I can say this,
that he got everywhere, in history and in space.
So I scraped him off with something like a spatula,
and then I took him off that thing like a spatula
with something like my finger, and then I undressed him
and ground him down (gently), and I wettened him
and mixed him up and kneaded him and folded him
and clothed him again, and then I filled in each of these
here holes with him to help make everything safe.

1 Collaboration

At 4pm Manning and I sat down to discuss the poem and his role in it. An imaginary wind buffeted and rattled the remote French farmhouse window like some sort of device, like a signifier of something trenchant and solemn. Manning said he was so excited about the poem that he was actually *rock-hard* as he put it, and what about I set it in a hotel room and sort him out with a Latvian stripper and half an ounce of good quality gak. And with that, quite matter-of-factly, he pulled his johnson out of his zoot suit pants to show me his predicament. His member (though my gaze, I can assure you, recoiled from it with more haste than a hand would from a hot coal) looked something like a monstrous jewel in the setting of the surrounding grey fabric of his trousers; or like, perhaps, a misplaced floral buttonhole that would have seemed less offensive had it protruded from the suit's lapel. It appeared to me that its grotesque rudeness buzzed against its, dare I say it, rather feminine beauty with a metallic ringing sound, but perhaps that was merely tinnitus brought on by the stress of the situation. I'd never known Manning to talk or behave in this way before. And even though it soon came to me that he'd been suffering from concussion after being hit full on the head by a lance in a jousting accident, and even though within a day or so he'd recover fully and return to his sensitive, and innately feminist self, I found that I always felt a little wary in his presence thereafter, for what I'd heard and seen that afternoon must surely have lain dormant in him for all the time I'd known him. And perhaps since then, I consequently feel a little less secure in the company of all my friends and acquaintances as well, of course, as in the company of myself.

II The Stage Is Set

Some weak, decrepit wind once sloughed off
a dismal place
and made of the yawns
of the wretched old men who once lived there
comes to a sorry halt over the land and expires disturbing
nothing.

*

Manning pulls the damaged machine out of its dive
just above the blind and dopey trees that panic only once
the danger's passed.

He hears himself laugh
like a mad Hun
and the washed skies lie all about him
thinned with the dreamt-up blood of angels.

Manning, his aircraft,
the flapping fabric of its torn wing,
the trees and the sky are all one and the same.
They each smell exactly of breath.
They are made of the same
finely patterned material,
part hard, part nothing,
of which every concocted thing is made.

Manning is most likely a poet. To his lovers he says things like:

I am rinsed through passion, my darling;
absolved, ruined; absolved, ruined.

He tries to gain height now,
he means to pull up and up
towards a cloud that looks exactly like a cauliflower

or an old woman striking a lofty attitude and lighting a pipe.
Once inside the cloud
he'll continue to climb, using it as cover
as he hungrily re-gathers the potential
energy of altitude.

But though the aircraft's wings judder as though buffeted
by wind,
the propeller only grasps hopelessly, pitifully over and over,
like the hands of desperate children,
at the completely meatless air.

*

Back in the officers' mess
where I've put him
(I own him very much
as some people own bees),
Manning lights a thin cigar as a joke
and smiles at me
between puffs and bouts of coughing, daring me to allude to it.

The cigar is only a smokescreen though,
its smoke stands in for a hopeless ghost, all airs and graces.

III Does a Filmic Wind Tousle the Photo-Real Grass?

It does.
The ho-hum flies can barely be bothered to move their wings
to fabricate their buzz.

They use their mouths instead.
They make their buzzing
with their long black lips which consequently
blur at the tips
so it looks as if a tiny flapping fly alit
on each proboscis.

*

Enter Dr Manning with Marcie and me and you on a cliff-top path.

(Marcie and I are walking just behind the doctor
and are holding hands secretly,
you are bringing up the rear, picking blackberries
and then scampering along the path to catch up with us).

Dr Manning:
How convenient, then, that I should find
the reflection of my own self so arousing,
that I should be quite so enthralled by the sweet, up-market stink
of my smart papery hum.

Fact is, I can't say if Manning has an actual moustache.

Sometimes he does,
sometimes he doesn't.
Sometimes he doesn't,
sometimes he does.

The oscillation between having
and not having
can occur many times

in a single humid day
when the stuff of which we're made
and the material that surrounds us
become so similar in consistency
that we begin to lose
our definition
and to dissolve, or at least to fear it!

Also, the moustache
that Manning sometimes wears might be fake,

or alternatively, the doctor being, in common with us all,
spurious (or cooked-up as he puts it),
it might be doubly fake.

(I should mention, that I, as well as Manning as it happens,
have a powerful antipathy towards so much
that is nowadays labelled 'surreal',
perhaps because of the promiscuous availability
of 'unlikely' juxtaposition,
or the hideous banality of another's dreams.

But there are elements of his story to which, I admit,
that facile description seems inexorably drawn,
much as a magnet is drawn to cheese
in the kind of easy-peasy panto which we both so abhor.)

Allow me,
under the tall ships and all their lugubrious weight,
and the cannons and ropes and what-not,
the bent sea was absolutely
wet-through, *sopped right out to the gills.*

What hurts
more than anything
is how I watched it lie brazen under the sun,
creaking under the lightness too
of my impossible gaze

at the very same time
as Manning was unconsciously growing an
immeasurably small volume of facial hair
right under the nose of my mother,

who sat in the actual Inn,
breathing him in,
breathing him out,
breathing him in.

My old mum Merle who, I might add,
had always laughed so dismissively at moustaches,
as people of her social class
and in that lukewarm historical moment, always did.

In the courtyard
the fading evening light walks about aimlessly,
looking at the bushes,
looking at the expensive cars,
and then back at the bushes
and then back at the cars,

in its hand,
a glass
with a tiny bit of completely melted ice in it.

Wherever you drill into the world
you'll find its richness, dum-de-dee,
said Manning, and he ate another one
of my yellowy salted peanuts and lit a smile.

IV Denmark Brochure

The mood is polite, facetious.
Manning himself, disordered, facticious.
The average colour, purpley-beige

except when it's dark. (Forgive me, but
all of us, we did look up at the night sky.
We saw behind the day's

blue curtain – saw the terrible workings!
It seemed so bored with us!)
According to the intro (and why not?),

the average temperature is coldish,
depending. The sky, humdinging.
Geography, nice, alien,

peninsularic. Penguins, erroneous.
The sea, blank, made quite crispy
with say-so. Manning, popped,

avoidant. Marcie, ghosted, jizzed, lit.
I could go on. Beasts don't even
glance at a smashed moon.

v Manning in the Rock Garden

Chorus of the small stones: *We, then, are the mealy stones,*
our weight untrue, our authored heat curdles our manners.
Listen to our voices. Count us out. Count us in.

Forgive me. The dreamt, having no bodies
are unaffected by alcohol. The booze goes right through 'em
without consorting avec the dry scaffold of their sticks.

Bein' in some way, shall we say, *ill*, Manning the Stone
found himself born, found himself, ahem, dumped.
He can look at his actual concocted body.

He can photograph his itchy feet on the iffy ground.
He is pregnant, bone-stuffed. He carries himself in his middle
that's as stiff as a bubble.

He will be an old man never having been slitted. (I made that.)
(I have scribbled up the all of us.)
Myself, I daubed up inside myself in colours

appropriate therein. Manning is concerned that in the long run
this trick of ours don't work.
Forgive me, but we are absolutely cunted, absolutely coined.

VI Out Here in the Future, Everything Is Doubly Suspect

Manning, oh Manning! Oh! shouts the lovely she-alien, her delicious tentacles gesticulating madly, her voice like that of a whale. Manning looks up at her. He feels shame at his detachment just at the moment of the creature's joyful panic. How strange, he thinks, to find convergent evolution has produced such similar and complementary genitals on so many diverse planets. And how predictable, somehow, that every high-end creature should orgasm so similarly, and that his charm (we know he has it) as well as his innate physical skill should function so effectively when deployed on hyper-evolved vegetation, thought-stones, buzzing grey pools of intelligence or mollusc-type beings. Manning's Plexiglass helmet has begun to steam-up on the inside. The oxygen-rich atmosphere he breathes is unlike the octatron's, so one of them was obliged to wear the helmet while the other could safely inhale their own home-gas selected from the comprehensive menu available from room service and then fed through tiny vents into the plush, retro-styled cabin suite. Manning, as ever, had been the gentleman and donned the headgear, but now he appears, to the exhausted, subsiding octatron, like nothing so much as some comical, orb-headed creature. Then, with a gentle, and, to Manning's ear at least, maternal laugh, she takes the heavy white ball of his helmet in a still partly engorged tentacle and kisses it. *Oh Manning, how ridiculous you are, though I do believe I love you!*

VII *I am lordly, puce and done,*

but enough about me, Manning says
as he adjust his tights under what we take for a moon.

There's a cascading swagger,
everything is joy in a thin strip:

Forgive me, the trees themselves
are morose rather than lightweight, the sky is certainly lit.
The ground bows down like a dumpty stone
quite free under its own buff
beneath the undressed pomp of its own boff,
and Manning laughs a luvvy laugh beneath a stony arch.

Marcie is all light of course and buzzing honey,
though quite as quiet as my open hand
and my old forgotten blood
who sings to himself
as he trundles about
picking up oxygen
spending it wisely
driving the pump that pumps him round
picking it up again
spending it wisely
singing the red corpuscle song.

The made-bees are quite as quiet as the blown-mice
(all my house is glass),
and Marcie is just about as clean as any window
ever was.
No so sorry dirt at all for me to make my home in.

VIII *Don't talk to me about ghosts,*

Manning yelled with a laugh
as the prop juddered to a halt
and the Le Rhône engine let loose
an ostentatious culminating 'BOUM!'

Manning then swung elegantly down
from the Sopwith Pup cockpit,
walked around the wing,
came to a mock-shocked wobbly stop
and with his mouth ajar stood
quite motionless before me
on the upper-class and foppish grass.

A little while passed,
until it became quite evident to me
that he had either forgotten his lines
or he pretended to have forgotten them,
or, as I now firmly believe,
he was pretending to have forgotten lines
that he never actually had.

2

So, as I say,
there he positioned himself
as the light began to slowly fold itself away
into the dark's sober briefcase,
and all the while his expression remained
as blank but also as disarming
as that of, say, a turnip.

As I stared back at him,
as I returned post-haste
his stare, though now bedecked
in the splashy garb
of my own unexciting boat race,
I began to feel myself subjected
to the first in a long procession
of differing emotions
which would proceed to march
through my consciousness, saluting
in the fashion of squaddies
who process past their king.

3

The first emotion I entertained (as one might
entertain a shy and unassuming guest at tea)

was a mild embarrassment at his behaviour.
Then, as time went on, I became increasingly

more mortified, until, out of all that
itchy awkwardness

there sprang a fragile and unexpected shoot
of mirth as a silky stem

might rise proud from a stimulated bean.
And as that bean's

associated root bored its fidget way
down into my ticklish mind I found I must

soon produce a twiggy cough whose purpose
was to camouflage a raspberry-like splutter

behind which pressed a proper, full-blown
belly-laugh.

4

I entered next,
step by hesitant step,
a state of respectful awe,

not just at the fellow's gall,
not just at the fact he had
the wherewithal

to hold his pose,
but at what seemed to be
the dreadful weight

of that which his dumbness
seemed so eloquently
to yammer.

And soon it was that I admit
I suddenly began to weep,
to bawl, to cry

not as I have ever caterwauled
before or since but silently
as though a sliding sluice had lifted

and let the pity that I felt
for Manning and which had
backed up all this time inside me,

pour from my eyes and nose
and mouth and ears in a
monstrous waterfall of

amalgamated tears each single
one of which stood in for some
specific incidence of misery.

And as the tears flowed
so freely from me, as though
a distraught torrent burst

from a busted dam, an absurd
and yet unnerving fear began
to run along its boiling side

like a Schützenpanzer halftrack
rattling on the tarmac
of a barely moonlit,

barely flak-lit, near
pitch-black Ruhr valley road.
A fear that the pressure of those

backed-up tears had for all
these years powered
a rusty dynamo

that had furnished me with just
enough get-up-and-go to rise
each day from my bed, and that

once the reservoir was spent
I might never summon
enough spirit to do so again!

5

So finally it was that a bitter little dread began
to gather as a vapour in the near-emptied
bladder of that sorrow. An anxiety that I must
surely neither move nor speak and break
this spell he'd cast. And it was only many
minutes after darkness fell, to the extent that
his form had been entirely obscured for
a substantial chapter of time, that I felt able
to creep backwards out of the scene and away
as the world's alternate, piddling and barbarous
truths came down upon me as a dawn.

6

If you're anything like me you'll be wondering
if Manning was still there the following day.
Well the fact is that he was. There was no way
that I might ascertain if he'd stolen off to spend
the night ensconced in a hostelry or with some

confederate perhaps in a nearby abode, and
returned that morning with a hot and fortifying
breakfast lolling supine in his belly only to adopt
the same posture and open-mouthed expression
once again, but I can vouch with certainty

that when I found him in the field beside
his machine at approximately 6.15 AM, he
certainly gave the appearance of having been
positioned there right through the night,
as the dew which had formed on the grass

and on the Sopwith Pup had also formed on him,
and I was able to distinguish no tell-tale trace
of footprints leading up to his position.
I hesitate to mention this, but I swear I also
could detect a damp expanse on the front

portion of his britches, a darkened territory
which continued down the entirety of his right
thigh, as far as the top of his boot and which
might indicate his having remained in place
for many hours with no opportunity

to relieve himself since before his flight
began (though I should add that I wouldn't
put it past him to contrive even such an
outrageous diversion as a means of misleading
those of us who were his witnesses).

7

It was only when
some time had passed
that I espied a small boy,

perhaps nine years
of age or so,
stood some little

way away from me.
And when that boy,
who had also chosen

not to approach
Manning, decided
to take his leave,

I fabricated
from the material
of my presence there

a departure of my own
(as a Japanese might
construct a queer

though wanting toad
from a folded piece
of paper)

and when I returned
a second time,
at approximately noon

of that same day,
Manning and his aircraft
had disappeared,

as had any tracks
they might have left,
the dew having

long since dispersed
beneath the heat
of the sun.

In fact Manning
had left behind him
to my great and

continuing amazement
no trace of his presence,
no scintilla of suggestion

that he'd had any more
substance as my own
unravelling breath.

His failure to leave
at the very least a relic,
some trinket souvenir

through which I might
touch, through which
I might palpate my own

inchoate self excites me
far more than I am able
to express.

IX Enter a Ghost Smelling Minty

Holy-moly,
the ghost is only gaseous!

Though I might care for him
he is mostly ghostly,

largely see-through,
his weightless,

his ungravid, airy dong
will do nothing for the world

that's rude for it,
being made of earth and hot,

being all bark, all bite,
its stuff dug

from the horny old ground.
And who digged it?

Well, it did. Down there
in the filthy night. Just saying.

*   *   *

The Common Quail

I heard this great story the other day.
At least I'm pretty sure it was a great story,

and I think I heard it the other day.
Actually, I'm almost certain it was great

because I remember thinking, wow,
now *that* is a great story, and also

I'm pretty sure it was the other day
because I remember it was raining

and it was certainly raining the other day.
You know what, I really want to say

the story had a quail in it, but then
I also really *don't* want to say it had

a quail in it. Those feathers that a quail
has, that brown and beige plumage looks

so *right* in the context of the lingering
atmosphere of the story, but also viewed

another way it just seems so *wrong* with
it's *One Two-Three* call, and that kind of

roundish shape quails have – I don't know,
I just can't be sure either way. You know

that thing when you say to your friends
in the pub how you read a fascinating

article about our education system in
the West, and why it's so totally fucked,

and they go like, 'Wow, what did the article
say?' and you realise you can't remember

a single thing it said, except the residue of
that feeling of revelation you experienced

when you read it is still with you, and maybe
it's *that* that's the important thing.

The Lawn Sprinkler

The sprinkler's simple engine
that sputters through its repetitive routine

is powered by that water which
it distributes; just as the thickness of the tongue's

compelled to clever flutter
by those words which, as they pass over it, it speaks.

First off,

take note of my bespoke rabbit-folk,
pale, no meat on 'em (a transient enthusiasm)

as they burst from squiggly silos,
nibbling, nibbling, nibbling, liebling. Nibbling.

Then see how my consort bod escorts me
in its tight suit like a goon, and look how I leaf

so slowly through your autonomous scent
in the labyrinthine library of your presence.

This world is like edible earth to me: edible, certainly,
but full in the sense of crammed.

Me, I am but a pin – sharp, slid into it, new; or I'm old,
a blunt socket that receives existence's

three-pronged plug that sucks my polished electricity.
(I fill myself also, as a dog fills its wallop.)

Me, I'm the national anthem of somewhere shaky.
You, you're as neat as a particle.

I don't particularly mean you to touch me exactly.